ELEMENTALS

poems

Bradley McIlwain

Elementals
poems

Published by: In Our Words Inc./inourwords.ca

Editor: Cheryl Antao-Xavier

Layout Design: Shirley Aguinaldo

Cover Image: *Sunset over Brooklin, Ontario*
            by Bradley McIlwain, 2014

Author Photograph: Gregory Dru

Library and Archives Canada Cataloguing in Publication

McIlwain, Bradley, 1985-, author
        Elementals : poems / Bradley McIlwain.

ISBN 978-1-926926-53-7 (paperback)

        I. Title.

PS8625 I475 E44 2015   C811'.6   C2015-905265-3

DEDICATION

For my parents, Paul and Carmela, and my sister Brianna, for all of your undying love and encouragement.

To my friends at the Brooklin Poetry Society, with whom I have shared many of these and earlier poems — you have been there from the first draft to the second cup of coffee! Thank you for your creative spirit and treasured discussions.

To my friends and colleagues at the University of Toronto, iSchool in 2012-2014, where some of the poems in this collection were composed, between classes and coffee breaks, such as "Peter Pan," written outside the Thomas Fisher Rare Book Library.

To Brian and Mike for our early commutes and watching the sunrise over Lake Ontario. Brian — I will never forget our 5:30 a.m. conversations over coffee and heavy metal! Mike — you are forever the Crossword King! Thank you both for your kindness.

To all of my amazing friends and family, this collection would not be possible without you. Thank you so much for your continued support and inspiration!

ACKNOWLEDGEMENTS

Thank you to the editors of the following publications where these poems first appeared:

"Ad Astra" first appeared in the *New Verse News*.

"Reunion" first appeared in *The Open Mouse*.

"Sailing" first appeared in *Platform Magazine, Issue 13*.

"Superstition Mountains," "Witching Hour" and "Storm Watch" first appeared in *Wilderness Interface Zone*.

"Tightrope Walker" first appeared in *Wanderings Magazine*.

"Dear Mr. Poe" first appeared in *Crossing Baldwin*, The Brooklin Poetry Society Inaugural Anthology, (Beret Days Press 2013).

CONTENTS

Introduction

At some point in our lives we all look up to the stars. How many times have we wished silently to the sky? Envisioned our dreams reflecting back on us from the vast swirl of constellations embodied in the fabric of space?

For the first time last spring, I saw the magic of a meteor shower unfold over my backyard. I lay on the grass, sipping coffee, with a friend. It was May 24, 2014, shortly after 3:00 a.m., when suddenly there was a spark in the darkness: a golden fireball of light danced above the houses. In seconds it vanished into air. It left me speechless, enchanted. The experience inspired me to write the poem "Ad Astra," which is included in the *Fire* section of this book.

Soon after, I started recording other impressions or lessons from nature and how we interact with the natural world in our daily lives, from the song of a robin to brighten our day on the way to work, or the presence of a crow perched outside in the rain. They are part of our stories, too.

Elementals is inspired by our exploring of our sublime connectedness with nature, and how we navigate our own personal wilderness inside ourselves.

Many of these poems were written outside in the elements, or while seeking shelter from them.

Every so often we are reminded of how a walk down a wooded path can seem like stepping into a fairytale. I hope to capture the essence of those enchanted realms in this collection.

Our interaction with the elements, *Earth, Air, Fire,* and *Water* have the ability to transform our *Spirit*. These poems are like a trail of breadcrumbs — a magic bean stock — hopefully one that will inspire you to discover the mysteries of the natural world around you and, most especially, *in* you.

Enjoy!

Bradley McIlwain
July 23, 2015

ROOTS

I look out past the water
a sleepy horizon cradled
in the mouth of a crane

swooning to catch her
breakfast. The children
skip pebbles

and I see our reflection
rippled in the undertow.
Life was so fluid

when we hiked autumn
trails crunching beneath
our feet

wearing out tread on our
soles, worshiping golden
brown dirt

and the Ontario Red Fox
who followed in the bush
beside us.

Once, you pulled off your
socks, tiptoed
into the brook

like a ballerina
to feel life swirl
you in a tango.

Dance, you said.
The earth is our
harmonica.

SOUTHEAST

At harvest
a crow calls
at my back

Her voice
cracks with
mystery

scavenging
the remains
of a dream

Do I follow?

The woods
call from
their deep

the path
fading
into a
forest
of secrets

TABULA RASA

Stars shiver like sapphires
at the nape
of the night

In the snow
I search for
meaning

before it returns to moisture.
In winter
we are all

tabula rasa.

I want
to get back
to my blank slate

a sheet
of composition
blowing in a field

to capture
the music of
reeds

or a tree
living in
my guitar.

How many sunsets
has it seen to make
such beautiful sound?

FAMILY TREE

A pirate
hanging
in a field

so far from sea
one last
sunrise

worth
its price
in gold

SUPERSTITION MOUNTAINS

moonlight fills the desert
        like an old yellow
paperback
        ripe
with adventure

SUNRISE

A fox sighs
on the hillside

her eyes
burning ambers

Together
we share

the same sunrise
emerging

from a wilderness
of sleep

GROUNDHOG DAY

Sunrise
lifts the
eyes

forgets past shadows
casts new ones

wakes
dreamers
grasping
at stars —

coffee
drips
as I peel the shades
yearning

for my morning cup.
Ravens gather
across gray sky

Where do they fly
constantly
searching?

Today
bury me underneath
an ocean of flannels

I don't want to wake.
I reach for my pillow.
An army of frost giants
are camped
outside our
window.

BEAUTY

When the glass was full
neither of us
were short

on words
in those late
hours

your lips
parting
like a poet

imparting
the wisdom
of a firefly

making the night
worth dreaming
This morning

a song from the past:
a monarch
scratching

at my window
Some say
they may

become
extinct —
I don't believe them.

The world isn't beautiful
you said, *unless there are*
beautiful people to live in it.

MT. EVEREST

No, I have to go.
I have to go.
Your words fall

open like a flower
without water,
cracked

at the corners
of a smile,
preserving what

was left of your
edge,
here at the top of

the earth, where a
dream was like an
echo

carefully split into
halves.
Which half were you?

Courage carefully
stitched, you wore
your bravery

on your boots,
carried up 8,848 m
of ice and rock.

The camera survived
the one you brought
to summit

your last
moments
captured

in a struggle
of will, a sigh
of relief.

No one could
understand what it
meant to you,

what it had given —
what it would take
away

29,029 ft.
stirring in a blanket
of clandestine white

WITCHING HOUR

at midnight
bats
dart

through
streams
of moonlight

glistening
like gypsy
moths

above
mountain
tops

and dangling
dream
catchers

glimpsing
visions of
desire

between
meteor
showers

and lovers
seeking
comfort

I lay
beneath
the stars

breathing
their dust
like my ancestors

swallowed
by infinite
sky

11:15 A.M.

A train moans
long into night

my fingers
making love

to a fine cigar
on a balcony

pouring over
a warm beer

mourning the
death of stars

A moth my
only friend

TIGHTROPE WALKER

Watch as she walks
along the wire

so
delicately

carefully
care free

her fear
her will —

feet planted
unmoved by the wind,

pressing —
swaying and dangling

The horror,
the horror —

every step, cautious,
pressing —

every step, like life,
demanding —

My breath escaping
with the crowd

my heart pounds
in horror,

for the girl who
walks delicately

across the wire,
pressing—

one slip could be
fatal —

I hold my breath
then *gasp.*

SECRET

Snow again
a grey owl
poised

against the glass

I listen to
her tender
breathing

each note
a mystery

who is it
who guides her touch
teaches

my ears to listen
to the soul, if not
the heart?

FAMILIAR

We have crossed paths
black cats at sunset

shying from our own
shadows. Was it you

I saw drawing down
the moon? Midnight

blooms in my garden
like runes on bone.

We sprinkle red brick
dust at the door, ward

ourselves with magic
stones.

Crows carry our past.
In your eyes, another

path, an otherworld.

STURGEON MOON

A wolf cries
awakened
by a palette

of light —
on a wooded
path

the taste of
a first kiss
blossoms

ENCHANTMENT

Where is the
frog prince in
Monet's

Water Lilies
or the young
maiden

waiting
beyond the whistling
reeds

whose lips
I can never
reach?

FIRE

DREAMER, 1985

ghosts
dance (Lakota)
in your kitchen

we clink glasses
listen to Jim

break on
through!

so many doors to kick open

how many times
have we wanted
to let loose our B-sides?

We are only 30 once
and Paris is so real
on half a bottle of Bordeaux

I hear the music
guiding me down *Love Street*

Jim singing from his grave
at Pér Lachaise.

Even in sleep hearts beat
and in the mirror dreams
are closer than they appear

dancing with my inner
Shaman.

Poetry and Spoken Word

Quarterly Readings and Performances

Winter Edition: December 18, 2018

Renée M. Sgroi

Patrick Meade

Kerry Craven

Jenny Sorensen

10 min break

Elise Kubsch

Codrina Ibanescu

Sacha Farrell

Andrea O'Farrell

10 min break

Gwen Tuinman

Bradley McIlwain

Theresa Donnelly

Barbara E. Hunt

AD ASTRA

A wolf sings
out my back gate
where does he go
at four a.m.?

The undergrowth
is cool, calming.
Tonight, we are
both prey

to the sky gods,
hungry meteors
dripping from
the womb

a golden apple
waiting for the
sleeping hero
to awaken

REUNION

Once, at a wedding,
I saw you

after a long absence
and a few glasses of

red

the colour of your
gown in moonlight;

on the balcony
I stumbled

undressed your eyes
with my heart

Do you remember the
murmurs of butterflies

nestled in a garden
of jasmine flowers?

NASSUA ST.

Your body sways
between doors

heaven and hell
scraps of paper for a pillow.

Exiting a bookshop,
you ask for cigarettes —

I had none.
You liked my scarf

it looked so warm.

SEVEN OF PENTACLES

On warm evenings
you come to the garden
each kiss a broad meadow

deep and unending
full of lilac and sage
enough to make the new moon jealous

Even crows are envious
of love

fussing over roses
at your back gate

When it doesn't rain
lightning tangos across

the valley
when love

dangles on your clothesline
like a firefly

close enough
to catch

NOCTURNE

In my bed,
I inhale what is mine
and what is not mine.

Each night a harp rises
and falls in one breath:

lovers
lost in lustrous rhythm
under a mirror of stars

Dream of Lady Mary Wortley Montague

Vienna — salt and pepper stone,
your residence

at the emperors house — drinking
under silk and

velvet canopies, lush bedrooms
where you wrote

me letters, peering out your window
into golden gardens

picking poems from fruit trees — the
nightingale in your

throat singing reasons for sustaining
youth; the seven

wonders you died to touch, learning
life in cobblestone

archways, Turkish baths and baroque
temples

Mozart was the key. The magic of ruins,
the spool of a bard's

lace unraveling the city walls around you,
sampling what grows

                          just beyond the soil.

TREKKING

Water ripples
in the soles
of our shoes

life's essence
propeling us
forward

what if —
we could be
like spring?

Let worry
melt away.

The sun
exposes
even the tallest shadows.

We follow
footsteps
over frozen creeks

searching
ourselves
in pebbles of a tired dream.

GOODBYES

when we moved
I remember how
the moon was full

we drank coffee in
the kitchen— crows
crying at our window.

SAILING

Looking out I expect to see you dock,
pull up to our cabin on the lake,

ask me to dance; but the bulrushes
whisper nothing, no repose for safe

return; the temper of the wind has
stilled, unwilling to share intentions

or give fair warning, but the clouds
don't lie, even the sea turtles have

left their shallow beds — bad weather
hangs in the western sky — waves will

break, and air will crack. It's getting
late, and the whitecaps have turned

against the tide. Still — no sign of you
at the harbor.

MELODY

July
rain

drains
all day

off of
eaves

easily
as

a lover
or

guitar
string

as I sip
voodoo

lemon
peeled

passion
tea

waiting
for

lightning
to

strike
twice

SPRING CLEANSING

Crows
chant
at your kitchen

to brewing
K-Cups
and icicles

shifting
on tired
eaves.

You crack
a window
air out bad

spirits
who moaned
all winter

let them free
so we can breathe
again

Lake Ontario
melts away
our fears

ferries us
in a dream
bewitched

in morning dew

STAY

I will go down to the forest
at sunrise

with my shadow taller than
the tree line

until my heartbeat breaks at
the riverbed

to the slow steady stream of a
happier dream

with the woodchuck, making
music in the trees

trying to become grounded.

You are leaving again today
for the shipwrecks

in Georgian Bay, where ghosts
rattle from their restless hulls

anchored as shackles on your
feet.

The journey home is fathoms
deep, but I need sleep.

I will leave my boots at the door
wash my face and palms.

I will go back to my poems, try to
navigate my True North.

Later, I will return to the woods,
dig my nails in the earth
unearth some hidden meaning.
Stay —

Don't you hear the woodchuck
Singing?

AFTER THE ICE STORM

Do you remember the woods
forgotten amber frame?

I searched the skin of a poplar
tree

brushed the snowflakes from
its whittled skull

to gaze the centuries of veins
How many rings do we count

before our stories
become timeless?

STORM WATCH
for Brian G.

Lightning.
A ghost-like stillness

descends over open
water.

Tornado weather.
From the window

you scramble to
recover the CD's

and boom box, but
Metallica is already

electrified. *Party on,
Garth!*

as silhouettes bloom
origami boats

paddling like ants
against the current.

PETER PAN

dream ends
      I wake to dawns
embrace

      still chasing
after
      your shadow

SPIRIT TALK

smoke rises
from a fresh

      cigar

where does
it go

chasing after
the old West

      wind?

an eagle rises
born from the

      ashes

of yesterdays
dream

VISION QUEST

A crow pecks
at last years
soil

what secrets
will she reveal?
last spring, my

neighbour found
an arrowhead
in her garden,

fragments of
a shared path.
This morning

a moon glows.
An Ontario Red Fox
yips

at my back gate.
I cut myself on
the past,

writing out a dream;
old gods demanding
sacrifice.

AWAKE

I

1:15 a.m.

The moon stands watch
guarding a garden of dreams.

Does she wait for me to enter?

A train sighs, chasing time
beyond my window.

Both have the same purpose:
destination

II

3:00 a.m.

My dog barks at my kitchen window.
Who else is there except my reflection?

On the counter empty teacups wait to
be needed.

I make a hot cup, sipping old routines.

In moonlight, memories taste like lemon
chai

WHEN YOU'RE WITH ME
for Katie

The moon captures
the wanderer's eyes

where do we go
slipping silently

into the sky? Smoke
rings from our cigars

are delicately formed.
We have practiced the

art of letting go —
brandy has an infinite

shelf life. The stars keep
us company as we dream.

What does this poem mean
at 4:00 a.m.?

These faded letters
from my dull pencil

more magical
when you are with me.

SPIRIT GUIDE

Up ahead
a fox waits

at the bridge
her golden

coat glowing
like a secret

daring me to
follow.

Beneath us
a frozen lake

groans. Who
will take the

first step?

SUMMIT

What does the mountain know?

So soft
so still

I almost forgot my own shadow
listening like a tree in the storm.

DEAR MR. POE

Pen in my hand
magic?

Poe
would think so.

Poem by divination.
Ink, blood thick

coagulates at
the fingertips.

I know a woman
with raven eyes,

have memorized
her song in scarlet.

I wonder:
can she hear my pulse

beating beneath
the floorboards?

VIGIL
for Martha

I pass by the old churchyard
moss covered graves of 19th
century ghosts, their names
since forgotten, disappearing
on stone

The wind blows northwest,
snow grips the headlights
heading out of town along
Highway 7A.

November reaches into my
heart, freezing all the locks.
I feel vulnerable with all of
this white space.

Was it snowing back then?
I don't remember. Sirens
still wake me from my sleep,
trying to find you in a dream.

I struggle like these dead
branches, the words from
my pen a forest
dry with grief.

I was too young to know
how much I missed you. I
am only now just starting
to remember.

Your smile always warmed
me. I want to believe you are
smiling down on me from a
vigil of stars

holding my hand like we were
kids. There is so much more
you had left to say.

Twilight shivers at my back.
The night is as gentle as glass.
I graduate in a few days.

Wish you were here.

CPSIA information can be obtained at www.ICGtesting.com
Printed in the USA
LVOW10s1053290416

485902LV00004B/15/P